Mostly True

Collected Writings
& Drawings of
Brian Andreas

StoryPeople
Decorah

ISBN 0-9642660-0-8

StoryPeople
P.O. Box 7
Decorah, IA 52101
USA
319.382.8060
319.382.0263 FAX

storypeople@storypeople.com
http://www.storypeople.com/

First Edition: *August, 1993*
Tenth Printing: *September, 1998*

Printed by the West Coast Print Center, Berkeley, California

*To my sons, David Quinn & Matthew Shea, for reminding
me to be fearless & fierce for those who will inherit the
future, & most of all, to my dearest Ellen, for reminding
me to sing with all my heart.*

Other books by Brian Andreas available
from StoryPeople Press:

Still Mostly True
Going Somewhere Soon
Strange Dreams
Hearing Voices
Story People

Cover Art: Brian Andreas

Mostly True

Introduction

The stories in this book began as hand-stamped stories on StoryPeople. At art festivals and galleries, many people stopped for a moment to read them, and ended up staying for hours, as we talked about all the stories in our lives. In the end, many of you said "I want them all. When are you going to do a book?"

Well, here it is. Mostly true. Buy it. Read it. Send it to friends. Use it to start a conversation. Throw it at your dog. Teach it to people from other countries and have them translate it. Sing your favorites to yourself in the shower. Ask your children to explain them to you. Explain it to them when you're in the car and they can't get away. When you meet someone new, have them read it to help you decide whether you want to spend any more time with them.

I was going to tell you all about why I think stories are so necessary for our world today. Why I think we need new myths so we can see the world as the strange and beautiful place it is. But you already know that.

I like art that admits to being a part of life. The moments I have with my friends and family are really all I need. I like to take them and weave them into stories filled with laughter and music and lunacy. And they <u>are</u> mostly true, but I'm not telling which parts...

I hope you enjoy them as much as I do.

With love,

Most of the stuff
I say is true because
I saw it in a dream
& I don't have the
presence of mind
to make up lies
when I'm asleep.

Presence of Mind

We lay there & looked up at
the night sky & she told me
about stars called blue squares
& red swirls & I told her I'd
never heard of them.

Of course not, she said,
the really important stuff they
never tell you. You have to
imagine it on your own.

Blue Squares

I never met
the Devil (yet)
but I imagine it's
a pretty scary
experience but then
again I guess that's
the point.

My uncle told me once
there were 3 rules for a
great opera. Make it loud,
wear flashy clothes & if
it's not going your way,
kill yourself.

It has no basis in reality,
he added. That's why I
like it.

Opera Man

There are Angels
everywhere you can
imagine. I saw
one hiding in the
closet in our
bedroom
once & I
invited her
out but she
said she
was
waiting
for a
friend

chomp!

thank you just the
same & next time I
looked she was gone

Are you a princess?
I said & she said I'm
much more than a
        princess

but you don't have
a name for it yet
here on earth.

More Than A Princess

what I'm mostly good at is sleeping, he once told me in confidence, but he added, I don't see much future in it.

There was a single blue
line of crayon drawn across
every wall in the house.
What does it mean? I asked.
A pirate needs the sight of
the sea, he said & then he
pulled his eye patch down
& turned & sailed away.

Crayon Pirate

I threw out
my hope chest
a white back

because it
was too big
to carry
around
with me all the
time, but I
still kept all
the blankets &
clothes. I just
dress in more
layers now & I'm
hoping to move to a
cooler climate soon.

O no, she said, you
can't say just any
old thing to the Wind.
Only the Deepest
Secrets will do

& also you must
not use the letter i

Deepest Secrets

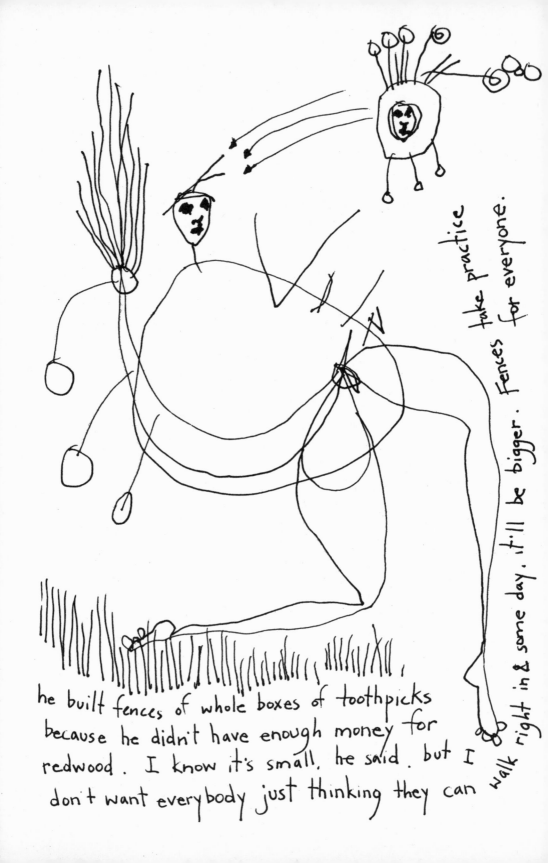

he built fences of whole boxes of toothpicks
because he didn't have enough money for
redwood. I know it's small, he said, but I
don't want everybody just thinking they can
walk right in & some day, it'll be bigger. Fences take practice. Fences for everyone.

I like Geography best,
he said, because your
mountains & rivers
know the secret.

Pay no attention to
       boundaries.

Geographer

My father used to carry a briefcase when he went to work every day before we left for school. Now. he stays at home & cooks us hot dogs for breakfast.

very important things

He told me the best
way to make coffee
was to add an egg,
so I did & he looked
at the strands floating
in his cup & decided
to have tea instead.

Egg Coffee

the next time the demons come, he said,
just wave your penis at
them. I can't do
that, I said.

Why not?
he said.

Well, I said finally.
because I'm American.

What's that thing? I said.
O, that's an oar, he said,
in case we hit a calm
stretch & we decide we
need more excitement

& also it's good for
slapping sharks.

Slapping Sharks

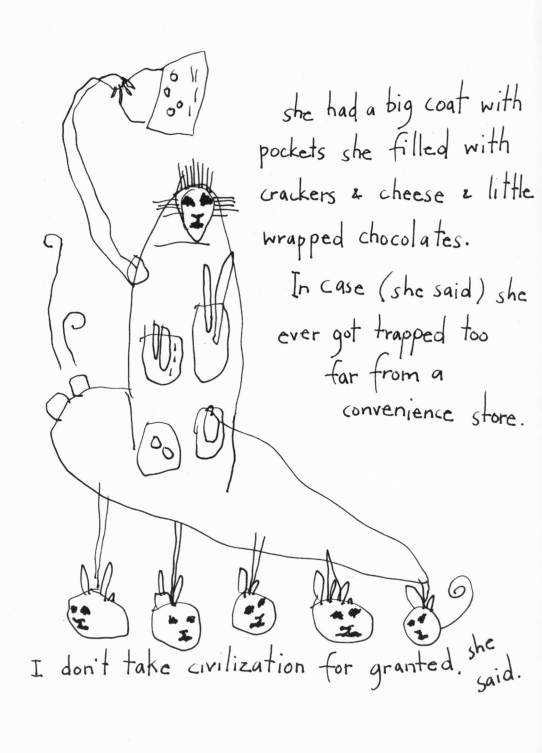

she had a big coat with pockets she filled with crackers & cheese & little wrapped chocolates.

In case (she said) she ever got trapped too far from a convenience store.

I don't take civilization for granted. she said.

A few said they'd be
horses. Most said they'd
be some sort of cat.
My friend said she'd
like to come back as a
porcupine.

I don't like crowds,
she said.

this is a giraffe bringing a
hostess gift of
juicy leaf
pizza because
he is so
tired of
there
never
being

anything
he can
eat at
these
functions

Your cat seems very
healthy, I said to her.

That is not a cat, she
said. That is a pig in
cat's clothing.

Pig Cat

I used to believe my
father about everything but then I had
children myself & now I see how much stuff
you make up just to keep yourself from
going crazy.

he said the hat
kept his soul from
drifting off & I
asked if he knew
this from experience
& he laughed &
said all his best
bits were from
National Geographic

National Geographic Hat

he kept her skin in the closet & brought
it out only for holidays so not to get
crumbs on it. Do you still love me?
she would ask at the end of each day
& he would hum her a song as
   he smoothed

away the

creases.

She said she usually
cried at least once
each day not because
she was sad, but
because the world was
so beautiful & life
was so short.

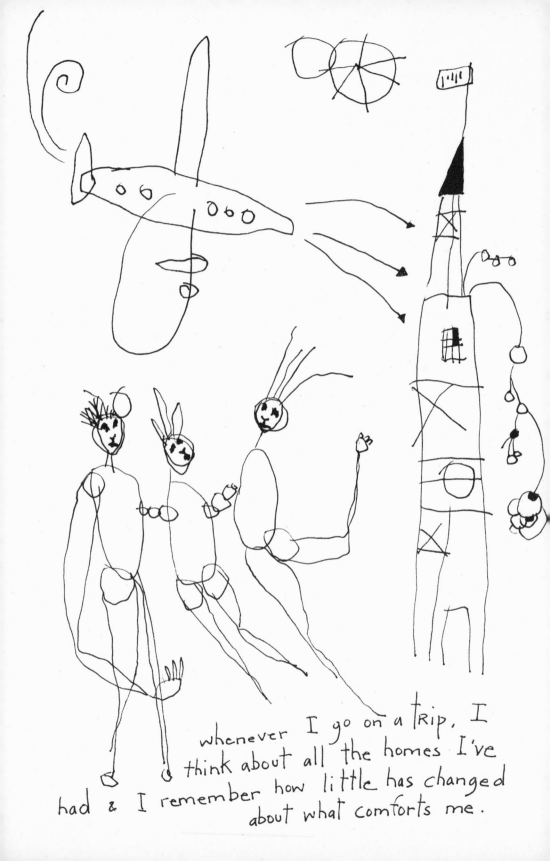

whenever I go on a trip, I
think about all the homes I've
had & I remember how little has changed
about what comforts me.

After his father
died, he carried
his life more
gently & left an
empty space
for the birds
& other creatures.

Empty Space

we
don't
have much
time, he said,
so I'll just
tell you about me.

The plumber was digging around
in the pipes & he saw something
shine in the muck & it turned
out to be the soul of the last
tenant.

He gave it to me & I said I
wonder how we can return it &
he shrugged & said he found
stuff like that all the time.

You'd be amazed what people
lose, he said.

The Plumber

He was always
a twin but he
kept the other
one hidden
under his
Stetson to
protect her from the
sun & the wind & the
stares of startled people.

I buried a nickel under the
porch when I was 8, she said,
but one day my grandma died
& they sold the house & I
never got to go back for it.

A nickel used to mean
something, I said.

She nodded. It still does,
she said & then she started
to cry.

Value of a Nickel

In her
dream, she
said, she
was a
bird who
fell asleep
& dreamed
she was a
man who
wore bright
colors & treated women
poorly & she asked all the
other birds what it could mean
& they all thought it was something in
the air & everyone agreed how lucky they
were to be birds & not men.

I used to wait for a sign, she said,
before I did anything. Then one
night I had a dream & an angel in
black tights came to me & said,
You can start any time now & then
I asked is this a sign? & the angel
started laughing & I woke up.

Now, I think the whole world is
filled with signs, but if there's
no laughter, I know they're not
for me.

Waiting for Signs

This is poison soup
to kill the bad witches,
she said.

How can you tell the
difference? I asked.

O, good witches are
very polite & say no
thank you. Bad witches
just die.

Bad Witches

I was never good at hide
& seek because I'd always
make enough noise so my
friends would be sure to
find me. I don't have
anyone to play those games
with any more, but now &
then I make enough noise
just in case someone is
still looking & hasn't
found me yet.

Hide & Seek

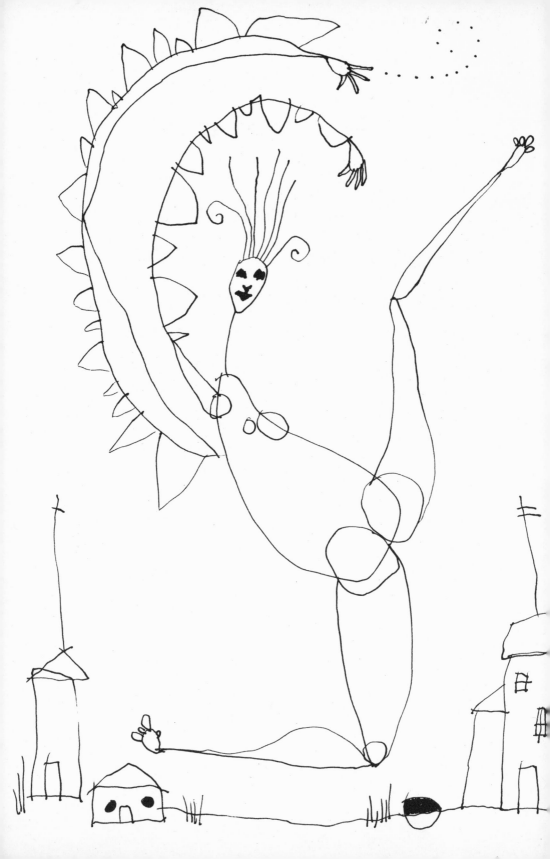

The first time her laughter
unfurled its wings in the wind,
we knew that the world would
never be the same.

Laughter Unfurled

I had a dream & I heard music & there were
children standing around, but no one was dancing
I asked a little girl, Why not? & she said
they didn't know how,
or maybe they
used to but
they forgot

& so I
started to
hop up &
down & the
children
asked
me, Is
that
dancing?
& I laughed
& said, no.
that's
hopping, but
at least it's
a start

& soon everyone was
hopping & laughing & it
didn't matter any more
that no one was dancing:

There are lives I can
imagine without children

but none of them have
the same laughter
& noise.

Laughter & Noise

Don't you hear it? she
asked & I shook my head
no & then she started to
dance & suddenly there
was music everywhere &
it went on for a very long
time & when I finally
found words all I could
say was thank you.

Unheard Music

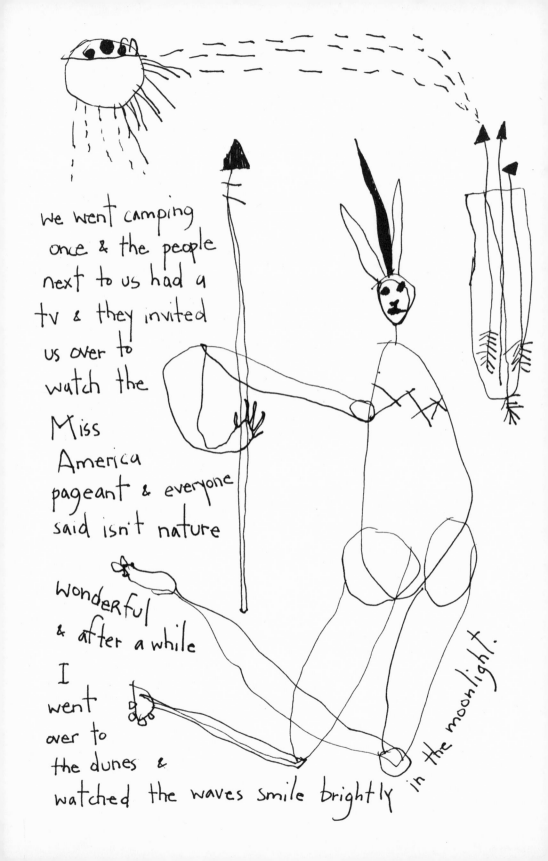

we went camping
once & the people
next to us had a
tv & they invited
us over to
watch the
Miss
America
pageant & everyone
said isn't nature

wonderful
& after a while
I
went
over to
the dunes &
watched the waves smile brightly

in the moonlight.

When I was young I told
everyone I had a twin sister.
One day, after we had been to
see the relatives, my mother
told me I was too old to play
that game any more. So I
stopped talking about her &
after awhile, she finally
went away.

But I'm grown up now & I
still miss her & I wish she
would come back.

Twin Sister

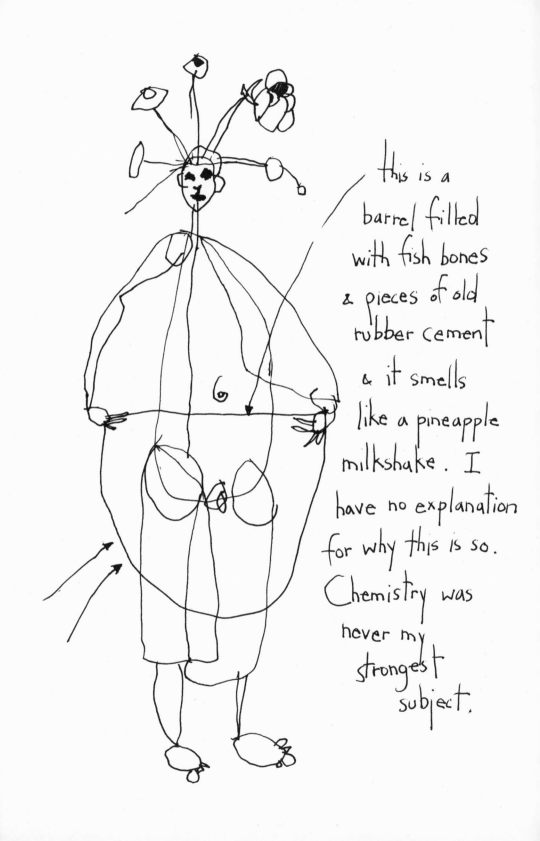

this is a
barrel filled
with fish bones
& pieces of old
rubber cement
& it smells
like a pineapple
milkshake. I
have no explanation
for why this is so.
Chemistry was
never my
strongest
subject.

My grandmother was big &
solid. My grandfather was
tall & thin. They looked
an unlikely couple.

I asked them once how
they ended up together.
My grandmother said she
won him fair & square in
an arm wrestling match.

My grandpa just smiled.
I let you win, he said.

Odd Couple

he carried a ladder
almost everywhere he
went & after awhile people
left all the high places to him.

It was a summer's
night & the smell
of the old rose bush
was as heavy as rain
& she asked me in

& I followed her
up those stairs till
morning.

Summer's Night

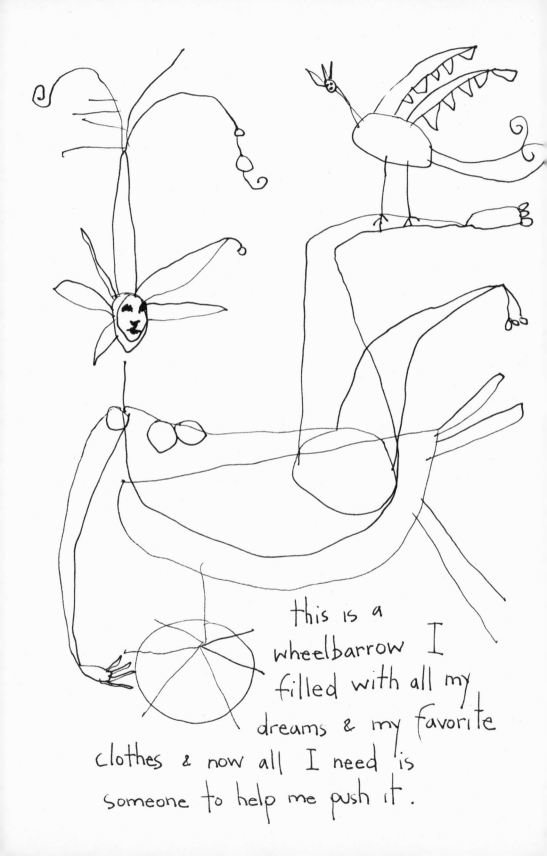

this is a
wheelbarrow I
filled with all my
dreams & my favorite
clothes & now all I need is
someone to help me push it.

She told me
once that the
year she went
to England
she painted
all her buttons
yellow so
she would
remember
what the
sun felt like.

Yellow Buttons

I spent a long time trying to find my center until I looked closely at it one night & found it had wheels & moved easily in the slightest breeze,

so now I spend less time sitting & more time sailing

When I first discovered
the moon, he said, I gave
it a different name. But
everyone kept calling it
the moon. The real name
never caught on.

Discovered the Moon

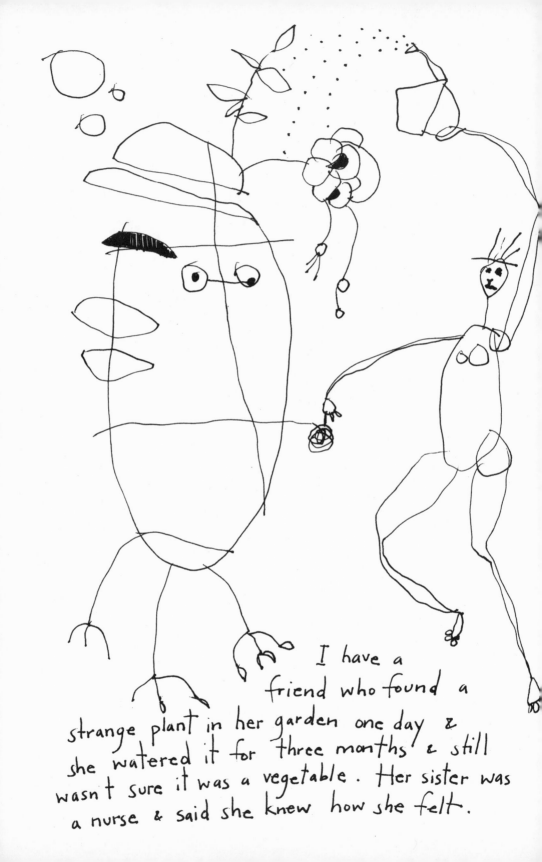

I have a
friend who found a
strange plant in her garden one day &
she watered it for three months & still
wasn't sure it was a vegetable. Her sister was
a nurse & said she knew how she felt.

I once had a garden
filled with flowers
that grew only on dark
thoughts

but they need constant
attention

& one day I decided
I had better things
to do.

Dark Garden

the feel of his spirit was too
old for most
people to
understand &
when he walked by
they would look up
& say O, the sun
went behind a cloud,
or, the moon must
be full & so he
walked for a long
time by himself
with no one to
talk to.

for a long
time, she
flew only
when she
thought
no one
else was
watching

Flying Woman

I'm old enough to wear red boots any time I want, she [said].
She wanted to be buried in them, but her son had them put her in taupe pumps instead.

she wore red all winter long so the ambulance could find her quicker if she fell in a snowbank & also it hides dirt. She had married early & had always been a pragmatist.

There are only 2
things I take
seriously, my aunt
said once. Laughter
& my digestion.
I'm too old to
bother with more
than that.

when they met the first time, he said he had
a brown thumb because
all his plants kept dying
& she laughed &
would not give him
    her number.

Every afternoon my grandmother
would have 2 chocolates with her
coffee. I asked her once how many
she thought she had eaten in her
life. If you laid them all end to
end to the moon & back, she said,
I'd be sitting right here even as
we speak

& then we celebrated her return
with an extra chocolate.

Chocolate Voyage

I have
always thought
that stars turn
into white birds
in the morning
light & sleep with
their heads under
their wings until
the dusk begins to
walk through
the streets.

She kept asking if the
stories were true. I kept
asking her if it mattered.
We finally gave up.'

She was looking for a
place to stand

& I wanted a place
to fly.

Place to Fly

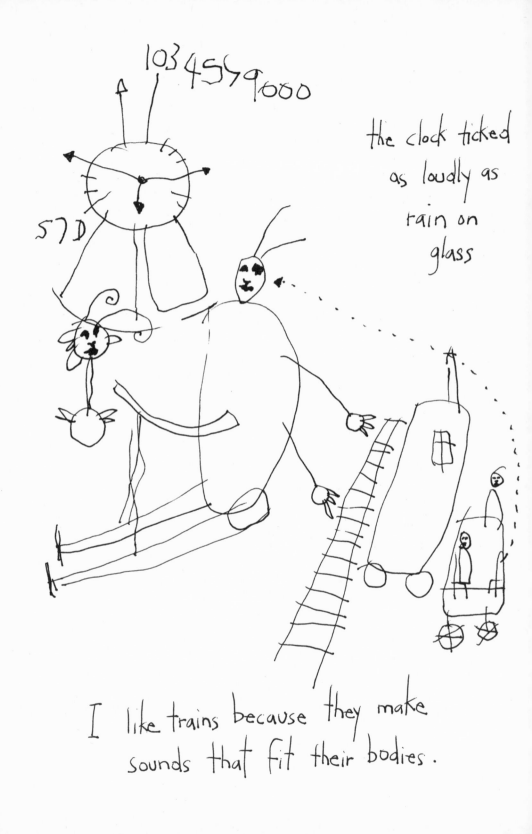

1034559000

57D

the clock ticked
as loudly as
rain on
glass

I like trains because they make
sounds that fit their bodies.

She waved at all the people
on the train & later, when
she saw they didn't wave back,
she started singing songs to
herself & it went that way
the whole day & she couldn't
remember having a better
time in her life.

Songs to Herself

her umbrella was
filled with rain she
had collected in her
travels & on hot summer
days she would
open it up for the
neighborhood kids & we
would splash in the
puddles
& then

Roar!
Roar!

it would smell like Nairobi or Tasmania
& later on we would sit on the porch &
eat ice cream & watch for tigers in
the bushes.

When I die, she said, I'm coming
back as a tree with deep roots &
I'll wave my leaves at the children
every morning on their way to
school & whisper tree songs at
night in their dreams.

Trees with deep roots know
about the things children need.

Deep Roots

he ran quickly with a sound like raindrops &
left his handwriting in all the secret places.

I found this one underneath the big yellow
rock in the garden. It said
this: watch out for
the little black
dog.

It can smell when you've had
hot dogs.

He wrote secret notes to
people he hadn't met yet.
Some of them aren't even
born, he said, but we live
in a strange neighborhood
& they will need help
figuring things out & I
won't always be around
to explain it to them.

Secret Notes

About the Artist

Brian Andreas is an artist, sculptor, and storyteller, who works with new forms of human community. He uses traditional media from fine art, theatre and storytelling, as well as the latest electronic technologies of computer networks, virtual reality and multimedia. His work is shown and collected internationally.

Born in 1956 in Iowa City, Iowa, he holds a B.A. from Luther College in Decorah, Iowa, and an M.F.A. in Fiber and Mixed Media from John F. Kennedy University in Orinda, California.

After years of adventure on the West Coast, he now lives with his wife, Ellen Rockne, and their two wild and beautiful boys in Decorah, Iowa, where he continues to make new stories for the StoryPeople, and, of course, for his next book.

About StoryPeople

StoryPeople are wood sculptures, three to four feet tall, in a roughly human form. They can be as varied as a simple cutout figure, or an assemblage of found and scrap wood, or an intricate, roughly made treasure box. Each piece uses only recycled barn and fence wood from old homesteads in the northeast Iowa area. Adding to their individual quirkiness are scraps of old barn tin and twists of wire. They are painted with bright colors and hand-stamped, a letter at a time, with original stories. The most striking aspect of StoryPeople are the shaded spirit faces. These faces are softly blended into the wood surface, and make each StoryPerson come alive.

Every figure is signed and numbered, and is unique because of the materials used. The figures, the colorful story prints, and the books, are available in galleries and stores throughout the US, Canada & the UK. Please feel free to call or write for more information, or drop in at our web site.

StoryPeople
P.O. Box 7
Decorah, IA 52101
USA

800.476.7178
319.382.8060
319.382.0263 FAX

orders@storypeople.com
http://www.storypeople.com